I Love Animals

Baby Animals

By Steve Parker
Illustrated by Ian Jackson

WINDMILL BOOKS
New York

Published in 2011 by Windmill Books, LLC
303 Park Avenue South, Suite #1280, New York, NY
10010-3657

Library of Congress Cataloging-in-Publication Data

Parker, Steve, 1952–
Baby animals / by Steve Parker ; illustrated by Ian Jackson.
p. cm. — (I love animals)
Includes index.
ISBN 978-1-61533-225-0 (library binding) —
ISBN 978-1-61533-231-1 (pbk.) —
ISBN 978-1-61533-277-9 (6-pack)
1. Animals—Infancy—Juvenile literature. I. Jackson, Ian, 1960– ill. II. Title.
QL763.P373 2011
591.3'9—dc22

2010032301

Manufactured in the United States of America

CPSIA Compliance Information: Batch #BW2011WM: For Further Information contact Windmill Books, New York, New York at 1-866-478-0556

Contents

Giant Panda Cub

A newborn giant panda cub is smaller than your hand. It is white all over, it has almost no fur, and its eyes are tightly closed. The cub grows quickly. By six weeks old, it can leave its den and follow its mother. By six months old, it is eating its favorite food, **bamboo**.

The baby panda is born in a den, cave, or hollow tree. The mother leaves it twice a day to look for food and water.

The female panda usually gives birth to just one cub, but sometimes she has two. She may have as many as eight cubs in her lifetime.

When a baby panda is hungry, it will cry like a human baby. The cub stays with its mother for over a year.

Panda Face!

Make a panda face from a paper plate and four black circles. Can people guess what you are?

Gray Wolf Cubs

For the first few weeks of their lives, gray wolf cubs stay inside their den, cave or **burrow**. They drink their mother's milk. Then they begin to leave the den and start to eat meat.

Wolf cubs are brought their first meaty meals not only by their mother, but by their father, too—and by other members of the wolf pack.

Howling Wolf

Wolves do not really howl at the Moon. They are simply telling other wolves, "I'm here!"

Penguin Chick

No baby animal grows up in a colder place than the emperor penguin chick. It is -58° F (-50° C) in icy Antarctica. This is colder than it is in a freezer. Luckily the chick has its father to keep it warm.

Who's Taller?

The emperor penguin is the biggest penguin. It is 47 inches (119 cm) tall. How tall are you?

Father penguins shelter younger chicks in their belly feathers.

The penguin chick cheeps and pecks its father's beak. This makes the father bring up food from his stomach for the chick to eat.

After two months at sea catching food, the mother penguin returns to her baby. Now the father can go off to feed.

Older chicks grow fluffy feathers. They huddle together for extra warmth in the icy wind.

Elephant Calf

A baby elephant has the world's biggest, strongest family to look after it. Not only does it have its mother, but also its older sisters, its aunts, and even its grandmother, who leads the whole herd.

The mother constantly touches her baby with her trunk. If she is busy feeding, an older sister or aunt "babysits" and keeps the calf out of danger.

Cool, Mom!

When a baby elephant gets too hot, its mother stands so that her shadow keeps the baby shaded and cool.

For the first year or two, the calf stays close to its mother.

The baby drinks its mother's milk for up to four years.

A young male elephant leaves the main herd when he is about 12 years old. He joins other young males to make a smaller herd.

Orangutan Baby

A baby orangutan is like a human baby, except hairier! It sleeps a lot, cries when it is hungry or frightened, and goes to the bathroom where it wants. The mother orangutan is very caring and protects her baby from predators, such as large eagles.

A baby orangutan may stay with its mother for as long as eight years.

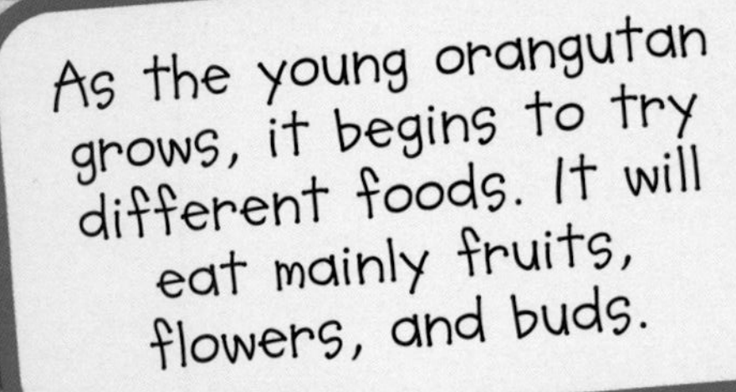

As the young orangutan grows, it begins to try different foods. It will eat mainly fruits, flowers, and buds.

Orangutans live in trees. They are good climbers. Their feet and toes grasp almost as well as their hands and fingers.

Great Ape!

The male orangutan is twice as big as the female. At 176 pounds (80 kg), he is the world's heaviest tree-living creature.

The young orangutan feeds on its mother's milk for three years or more.

Fawn

A baby deer is called a fawn. Its coat is covered in white spots. As the sun shines through leaves and twigs, it makes light spots on the forest floor—just like the spots on a fawn's coat. The fawn lies still and silent. Its mother stays nearby, feeding and watching.

The spotted coat blends in with patches of sunlight on the ground. This makes the fawn difficult to see.

Big Head!

A buck is a fully grown male deer. He grows huge antlers each summer. They fall off in late winter.

The fawn has huge ears, big eyes, and a good sense of smell. If a predator comes too near, the fawn jumps up and runs away.

The doe, or mother deer, visits her baby to let it drink her milk.

Kittens

A mother cat is very busy. She has to feed her kittens, keep them warm, lick them clean, let them climb all over her, and stop them from wandering into danger. She may have a **litter** of ten or more kittens to care for.

A kitten learns to crawl first. By about four weeks old, it can walk. A week later, it is running and jumping.

Popular Pets

Some years ago, dogs were the most popular pets. Now cats have taken over. How many pet cats do you know?

Kittens can recognize each other by smell, even in total darkness.

A kitten drinks its mother's milk for about eight weeks. It begins to eat other foods at three weeks.

Joey

A baby kangaroo is called a joey. For the first six months of its life, it lives in its mother's pocket-shaped pouch. Here it is safe, drinking her milk. Soon, the joey grows strong enough to leave the pouch and explore. If danger appears, it hops back in again.

A young joey is very shy. The first time it goes outside, it rushes back to the pouch after a minute. Soon it becomes braver and stays out of the pouch for longer.

The older joey still pops its head into its mother's pouch to drink her milk until it is almost a year old.

The mother kangaroo has to clean her pouch often, using her paws, teeth, and tongue. She throws out bits of dirt and fur that her joey leaves behind—and its droppings, too!

Hop, Hop, Hop!

Can you hop like a kangaroo? Keep your feet together, knees bent, and hands held up like paws.

When the joey is eight months old, it leaves the pouch and never comes back. It still stays near its mother.

Baby Otters

Many baby animals like to play—especially otter babies! They roll, tumble, and jump in the riverbank mud. Sometimes they have pretend fights. This is practice for when the otters have to hunt their own food.

Lazy Otters

After a big meal, an otter spends a day or two lying around in its couch, or den.

The otters stay in their burrow for two months. Then their mother leads them out to the riverbank, where they play and learn to swim.

By the time otters are four months old, they can catch fish, baby frogs, and waterbird chicks.

The baby otters grow a thick, waterproof coat that keeps them warm and dry in the water.

Seal Pup

The harp seal pup lives in the Arctic. This baby is surrounded by snow, ice, and freezing cold sea—as well as hungry hunters, such as polar bears and wolves. The pup lies perfectly still. Its thick, white fur keeps it warm and hides it in its snowy surroundings.

If a pup cannot find its mother, it wails and cries like a human baby.

Harp seals eat mainly fish, such as herring, cod, and capelin. They might try a snack of squid.

Deep Diver

Harp seals can dive 980 feet (300m) deep and stay underwater for half an hour!

The pup's fur is yellow at birth. It soon turns white. The pup then grows a new, darker fur coat.

The pup is only looked after by its mother for two weeks. Then she goes back to sea. The pup must learn to swim, dive, and catch fish—fast!

Read More

Fraser, Mary Ann. *How Animal Babies Stay Safe*. Let's-Read-and-Find-Out Science. New York: HarperCollins Publishers, Inc., 2001.

Fujikawa, Gyo. *Baby Animal Families*. New York: Sterling Publishing, 2008.

Williams, Garth. *Baby Animals*. New York: Golden Books, 2004.

Glossary

Bamboo (bam-BOO) A thick, woody grass with stems with a hole in the middle.

Burrow (BUR-oh) An animal home that was dug out of the ground.

Litter (LIH-ter) A group of babies born to a mother animal at the same time.

Predators (PREH-duh-terz) Animals that kill other animals for food.

Shelter (SHEL-ter) To guard an animal or person from weather or danger.

Index

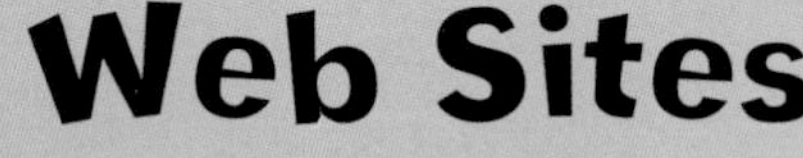

Web Sites

For Web resources related to the subject of this book, go to: www.windmillbooks.com/weblinks and select this book's title.